Chinese Pioneering Inventions Series

Dujiangyan

Edited by Li Chaodong

Translated by Xuemeng Angela Li

Books Beyond Boundaries

ROYAL COLLINS

China is an agrarian society. Chinese farmers can live and work in peace only if the weather is in favor of crop yield.

When bad weather occurs, farmers will run into their biggest enemies—floods and droughts.

During the Pre-Qin Dynasty, to fight against these disasters, large amounts of labor and resources were often mobilized through the centralization of state power to build large-scale water conservancy projects, which fully demonstrates the talent and wisdom of the Chinese ancients.

Emperor Yu
Tamed the Flood

Ximen Leopard
Controlled Floods

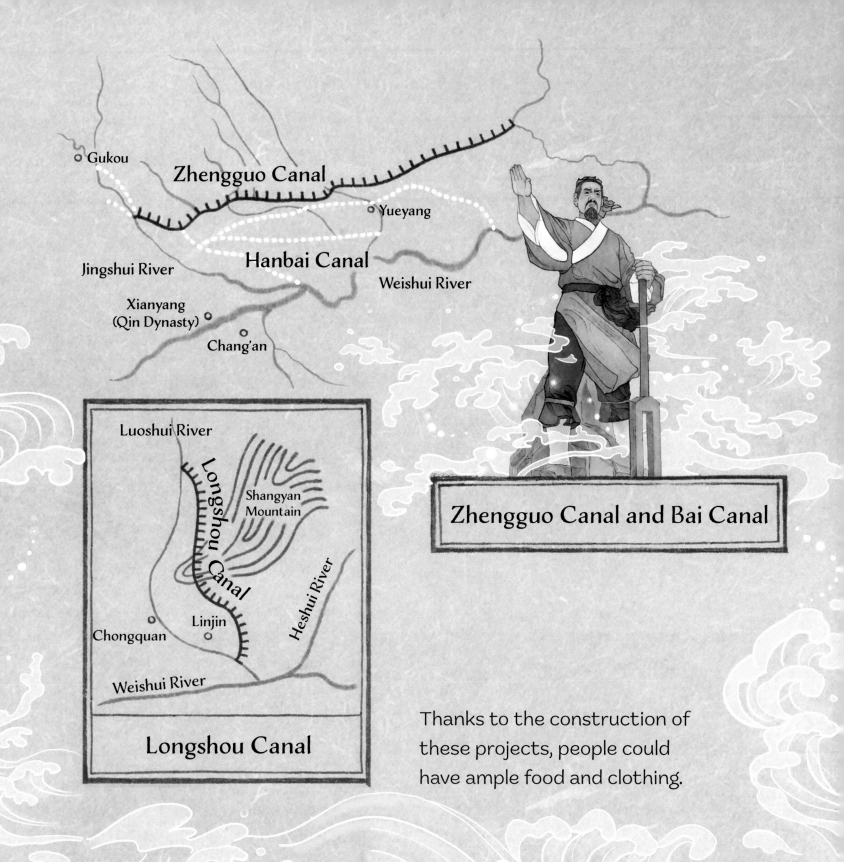

Gukou

Zhengguo Canal

Yueyang

Jingshui River

Hanbai Canal

Weishui River

Xianyang
(Qin Dynasty)

Chang'an

Luoshui River

Longshou Canal

Shangyan
Mountain

Heshui River

Chongquan   Linjin

Weishui River

Longshou Canal

Zhengguo Canal and Bai Canal

Thanks to the construction of
these projects, people could
have ample food and clothing.

Among the numerous water conservancy projects built during the Pre-Qin period, there is one magnificent and sophisticated project that has been continuously benefiting the Chinese for more than 2,000 years— the **Dujiangyan** (Dujiang Weir) project.

In ancient times, the people of the Sichuan region suffered from frequent droughts and floods and lived under difficult conditions. This was the case until Li Bing was appointed by King Zhaoxiang of Qin as the governor of Shu County during the Warring States period, which was more than 2,000 years ago from now. The people of Sichuan heard that their new governor knew astronomy and geography and thus went to seek his help together.

After promising the people a solution, Li Bing, together with his son, worked tirelessly on a river regulation plan. He drew on the experience of his predecessors, combined it with his investigation of the topography of the rivers in Sichuan, and eventually came up with an extremely creative construction plan.

North

Min River

Yuzui
(Fish mouth)

Convex
bank

Concave
bank

Outer
river

Jingang
Dike

Inner
river

Yulei
Mountain

Min River

Feishayan
(Flying sand weir)

Baoping
Mouth

Lidui

Miter dike

East

都江堰工程图
Dujiangyan Project Drawing

First, he asked people to build Jingang Dike in the center of the Min River to separate the river flow. The front of the dike was in the shape of a fish mouth and was thus called Yuzui (in Chinese).

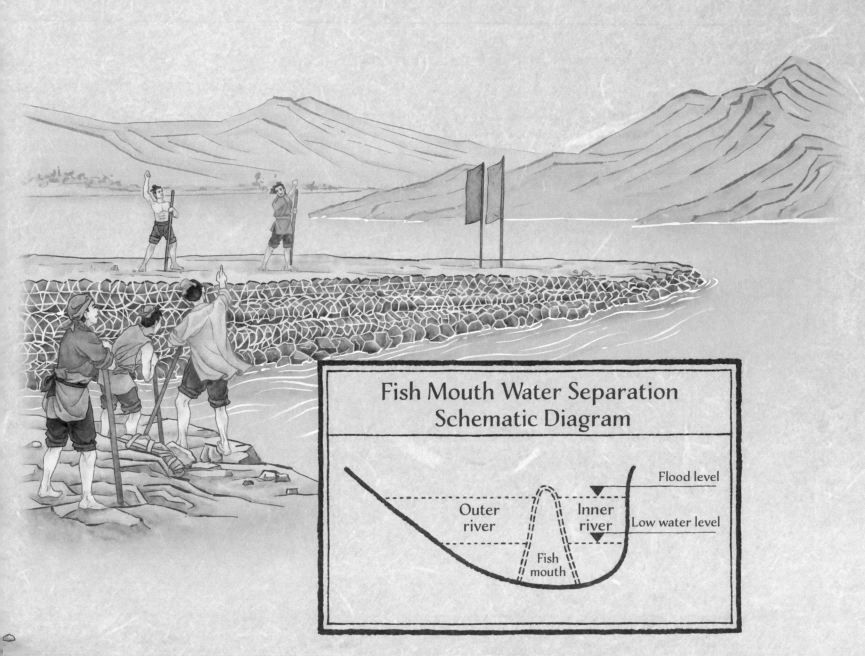

Fish Mouth Water Separation Schematic Diagram

Flood level

Outer river

Inner river

Low water level

Fish mouth

During the dike construction, the water flow was so fast that stones were washed away immediately after being thrown into the river. To solve that, Li Bing made large baskets using bamboo from local mountains. He filled the baskets with stones and then threw them into the Min River. Bamboo baskets were stacked one after one, which eventually formed a dike. The approach adapted to local conditions and put together pieces into a whole. How wise!

After that, people started to brainstorm ways to excavate Yulei Mountain to divert water into farmland. It was a difficult mission, but Li Bing came up with a good idea. He first set fire to burn the wall of the cliff and then diverted the river to pour on it, which created cracks in rocks and made them easy to cut.

Eight years later, the Yulei Mountain was finally dug into a gap, which is called Baoping Mouth. A very important scientific principle underlies this solution—thermal expansion and contraction.

Now that the river finally flows into the farmland, what water volume would be ideal? Li Bing asked several people to build some stone figures and put them on the bank of Baoping Mouth as a water measurement ruler.

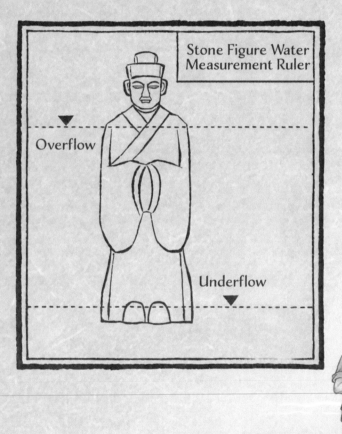

Stone Figure Water Measurement Ruler

Overflow

Underflow

As per Li Bing's assumption, the water level should not be higher than the shoulders of the stone figures, which would make the crops inundated; nor should it be lower than the stone figures' feet as too little water would expose the crops to drought. The stone figure is both practical and beautiful as a water ruler; many water conservancy projects built later have thus followed this practice.

Now everything is ready; how did they make the water behave?

When the water volume is high, they make the Yuzui (fish mouth) lean towards the right, which reduces the water volume flowing into the inner river.

When the water volume is low, they make the Yuzui lean towards the left instead, which increases the water volume flowing into the inner river.

What if the water volume is particularly low? Don't panic! People would use bamboo baskets to build a dike between the Yuzui and the convex bank, which enables the entire water to flow into the inner river.

But what if it's an extremely bad situation with no water in the river at all? Then people would really run out of solutions.

The reason for river cut-off could either be the low precipitation of the year or the destruction of water sources in the upper reaches of the rivers, which results in a significant reduction of water flowing downstream. To avoid such a situation, we must protect the environment, adapt to local conditions, and learn to live in harmony with nature.

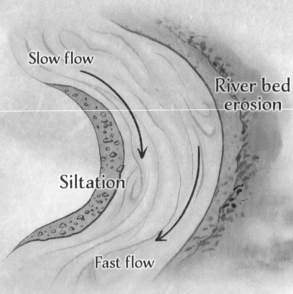

Slow flow

River bed
erosion

Siltation

Fast flow

The problem of water flow
volume has been solved, but
sedimentation still exists.

The river carries some sediment inside when it flows. When the water flow slows down, sediment will accumulate at the bottom of the river. If not cleared in time, it may block Dujiangyan in the long term.

Convex
bank

Yuzui
(Fish mouth)

Outer
river

Jingang
Dike

Concave
bank

Feishayan
(Flying sand weir)

Lidui

Therefore, Li Bing cut Jingang
Dike in the middle and built
Feishayan (Flying Sand Weir).
When the floor occurs, the
excess sediment in the inner
river has washed away.

After Dujiangyan was repaired, a downpour suddenly occurred one day, causing a rapid rise in river level. Local residents all ran up the mountain in a panic.

After they reached the summit, they found that the flood water below had surprisingly slowed down after passing Dujiangyan. The majority of it flowed away directly through the outer river, while a small portion slowly flowed into the inner river and reached the farmland to irrigate the crops without causing any damage.

After the flood occurred, drought immediately followed.

The blazing sun scorched the earth, with trees on the mountain withered to yellow. It was because of Dujiangyan that the crops in farmlands could keep flourishing.

Thousands of years went by, and Dujiangyan has been continuously guarding the farmland and farmers on the Chengdu Plain, making it a land of abundance.

After Li Bing and his son passed away, local residents built an ancestral temple for them, which is called the **Er Wang Temple**. Every year, many people come to pay respects and appreciate their contributions.

In 2000, **Dujiangyan** was added to the World Heritage List. Nowadays, the site welcomes many visitors from all over the world every day. It guides the visitors to experience the wisdom and power of the ancient Chinese people.

世界遺產·都江堰

THE WORLD HERITAGE
DUJIANGYAN

South Bridge

Qingcheng
Mountain

青城山

Hi, little engineer! Now, please follow this picture to tell everyone the story you just read about the Dujiangyan project with your mom and dad.

Chinese Pioneering Inventions Series

Dujiangyan

Edited by Li Chaodong
Translated by Xuemeng Angela Li

First published in 2023 by Royal Collins Publishing Group Inc.
Groupe Publication Royal Collins Inc.
BKM Royalcollins Publishers Private Limited

Headquarters: 550-555 boul. René-Lévesque O Montréal (Québec) H2Z1B1 Canada
India office: 805 Hemkunt House, 8th Floor, Rajendra Place, New Delhi 110 008

Original Edition © Hohai University Press

ISBN: 978-1-4878-1102-0

To find out more about our publications, please visit www.royalcollins.com.

About the Editor

Li Chaodong, born in 1963, graduated from the Department of History of East China Normal University. He is a famous education publisher in China. He has edited and published more than 50 sets of books. He has won the title of "National Leading Talent in Press and Publication" and "China's Annual Publication Figure." He is the Founding Vice President of the All-China Federation of Industry and Commerce Book Industry Chamber of Commerce, Vice President of the Fifth Council of China Book Publishing Association, Vice Chairman of Anhui Publishing Association, and Vice Chairman of Jiangsu Publishing Association.